How
To retire at the age of
25

PRITAM BAHADUR

Copyright © 2018by Pritam Bahadur
All rights reserved.
This book or any portion thereof may not be reproduced or used in any manner whatsoever without the express written permission of the publisher except for the use of brief quotations in a book review.

Printed in India.

First Printing, 2018

ISBN: 9781730712036

Kindle Direct

Publishing

www.kdp.amazon.com

Content

1. Let's talk — 5

2. What to do then — 9

3. The business — 16

4. Is it wrong — 20

5. Why to do — 24

6. Conclusion — 26

TO MY TEACHERS

Mr. Rahul Kumar Walia

Mr. Amit Yaduvanshi

Mr. Mohit Rathore

Mr. Vinay Kumar

1. Let's talk

I'm here to give you the answer of the question *"how to retire at the age of 25?"*

There are some steps.

Step 1: - Complete your School.

Step 2: - Get a good Degree.

Step 3: - Get a good Job.

BOOK IS OVER.

<THE END>

You might be thinking, "*are you crazy buddy? I didn't spend my money for this crap*".

Exactly, this is how it feels when you expect more and get nothing. Jobs are exactly the same, you had always expected more from it while studying but you know what, at the end you'll get nothing. And my friend you have spent your money, for that crap too. (In the form of school, college and tuition fees)

It's not like I'm saying that jobs are bad or you should not do it, I'm just saying jobs are for those who don't have ambitions, who don't want to live a luxurious life or who don't have any other option. I am saying this because, the salary you would get will only help in fulfilling your **BASIC NEEDS** not your **DREAMS**. But you might be thinking that I'll do job just to earn some money and then I'll start my own business but admit the fact my friend that job is a *Marshland* from where it is extremely difficult to bring yourself out. The more you try to leave the more you'll find yourself going deeper and deeper.

Now, you might be thinking, "*If Job is not the option, what I should do then? Should I start my career with a business? Then what business? And How?*"

Relax buddy, I'll answer all of your questions. But before asking *what* and *how*, you must ask *when?* When to start your career?

Look, from my experience if you start your career after completing your studies, say for at the age of 25, and practically if you want to earn really big, you need to be experienced and for that you have to give your first two to three years just to gain some experience and understand the market tactics, because it's not something what your teacher will teach you in the class and by this you'll definitely not be able to retire at 25. Rather I suggest you to start your career earlier, at the age of 18 or 19 right after completing your school. It will help you to be market ready before the rest of the students of your age. And once you come out of the comfort zone which had been provided by your parents, you'll realize how hard it is to earn a single penny and how much money of your parents you've already wasted on different stuffs. And then you'll be able to differentiate between non-useful and useful stuffs, which will lead you to invest your money on useful things like books, seminars etc.

But the problem is the mentality of our parents or you can say the mindset, due to the generation gap of course. They want us to study and to totally depend on it. They feel insecure for our future and that is why they want to secure our lives and in doing so they made our secondary choice the primary one – jobs. Do you remember, just to make us study they have lied so many times like, "just complete your 10th standard and your life will be great", then after completing 10th, "complete your 12th and there will be nothing to worry about", and then "only three to four more years you have to study and your life will be on a great track", but at the end there will be nothing but a 9 to 5 job is waiting for you. Do you really think that a simple job is enough to fulfill your **DREAMS**? If your answer is *YES,* then my question to you is *have you ever seen your school teacher driving their own BENTLEY*?

No? Why? Aren't they educated?

Of course, they are, but the only reason that they can't afford a luxurious car is, they are ONLY educated. They were fully dependent on the education system. The same education system which was invented to make us slaves and of course they have succeeded because today we study more and more and more to become a HIGHLY PAID SLAVE. I'm not saying that you should not study; education is must, because it teaches us the moral values, basic manners, and many theoretical things. But today only theoretical knowledge is not enough to make our life luxurious. Since the competition is increasing day by day, that even cracking an interview has also became one of the toughest jobs and even if you crack an interview you'll get a job and at least a job can't make you to get retirement at the age of 25. Just tell me do you want to live the same life as your parents and teachers lived? Do you want to repeat the same lines to your kids what your parents have said whenever you've asked them to buy something expensive?

If your answer is YES, then give this book to somebody else. But if your answer is NO, then tell me what you are doing now to make the difference?

If you're saying that I'm studying, then you are not the only one. So keep it in your mind "to make the difference you have to do something different".

2. What to do then

First of all, I would suggest you not to be a participant of the RAT RACE, in which everyone is running on the same track hoping for a different destination. Like if you ask your parents that have they ever played *HIDE & SEEK*, they'll say yes, and if I ask you the same question you'll also say yes, and if I ask you and your parents that have you ever read the nursery rhyme *Twinkle Twinkle Little Star*? You both are going to answer the question in yes. Which means neither the games nor the education system had changed; then how can you think that the same education will give you something different? And I don't know why but 90% of the Indian crowd is running behind Government Jobs. And most of them want to be an Engineer or a Doctor. People are crazy for getting the degree of B.Tech and they are wasting their money and precious time in the same which has already ruined so many lives. I mean just go and search it on Google that how many people are unemployed or working in *call centers* even after holding the degree, of your so-called B.Tech.

Do you know that unfortunately I was also a science student and in my 12th standard I had Physics, chemistry, Mathematics and Biology as my subjects. In short, I could be an engineer or a Doctor. But my mom wanted me to be an Engineer. So, like everybody else I also started preparing for the *JEE* (Joint Entrance Examination) *MAINS*. And after approximately four months of studying I was prepared for the examination. And then at the morning just two hours before the examination, I was sitting on the couch and reading a newspaper, and do you know what I saw?

THIS-

HOME

Number of engineering seats to go down by 80,000 this year

Manash Pratim Gohain | TNN | Updated: Apr 8, 2018, 10:42 IST

The above picture was of the day of my examination. After reading this I decided not to appear in the exam.

But many students of my class are still running behind this craziness. They had dropped their whole year for studying just to clear the examination and they are doing every possible thing to get the degree just to say that I'm an ENGINEER.

Do you know how many engineers graduate in India per year?

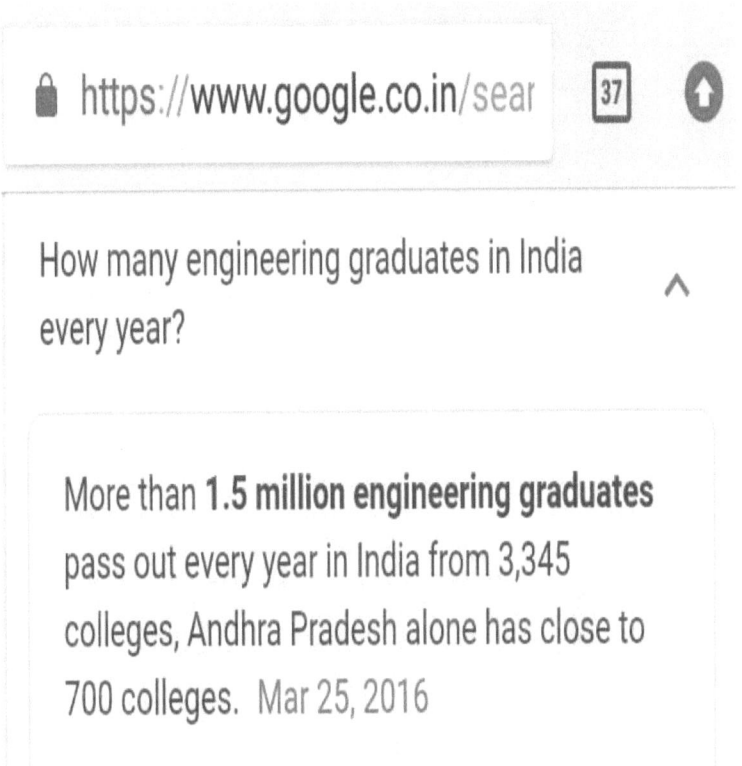

Wow! More than 1.5 million engineering students graduate per year that means more than 15 lakhs students graduate with a degree of B.Tech from all over India, despite the fact that Andhra Pradesh had closed 700 colleges. I know it's something to be proud of but producing Engineers is not a big deal today, it could a big deal in 1990's. And I don't think that this counting will going to decrease in the coming days, but now the question is how many of them are employed?

Guess. 50%?30%?10%?

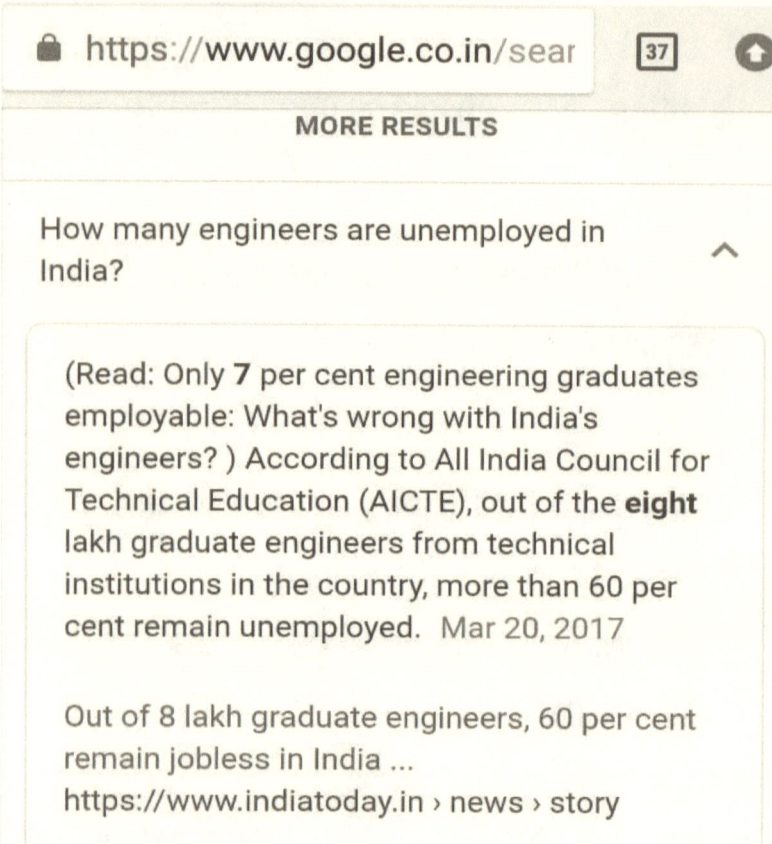

According to Google itself only 7% engineering graduates are employable not even employed and 60% are totally unemployed due to lack of skills, practical knowledge and of course lack of jobs. Indian engineers are engineers only on papers because they don't have any knowledge how to deal practically in life, they had only crammed the books to score good every time and many engineers are engineers just because their parents have asked them to study the course or field because they wanted to show off in front of their colleagues and neighbors. Sometimes it feels like I'm a Pokémon and my parents are the trainers and I have to fight with other Pokémons for nothing.

And it has become a myth in India that only education will make our life luxurious and successful. If it's true then I'm going to ask you the same question again, do any of your school teachers owned a *Bentley*?

Today the education is not an education; it has become a business module. Your tuition teacher earns much more than you think because they are not social workers and just tell me one thing are you an only student to them? They are doing business of probability if you will get good marks then you'll be on their list of good students and by showing that list they'll attract more students (haven't you saw the pictures of students who had scored good, outside the tuition centers?) but if you don't score good then you'll become a headache to them; of course a headache who pays.

If you're going to follow the same pattern, then you'll become a worker forever. You were a worker in school (worker for completing home works); you are being taught to be a worker in someone's company. So, instead of that why don't you work for yourself?

Now you're going to say, that everybody is working for themselves. But, no my friend, you must admit this fact that most of the people are working for their bosses, indirectly their bosses make them work, for completing their own dreams and for that they pay the workers under them. So indirectly you are considered as a slave who is working for generating money for your boss. But instead of that you must work for yourself.

Because money won't come to you if you run after it, but it will do come if you work for yourself. Since working for yourself will make you good, then better and then slowly and gradually it will make you excellent and my friend success always follow the excellence. (I didn't copied it from *3 idiots*)

And I personally believe that, working for your own self is far better than working for somebody else - bosses. I don't know why but our teachers and family had never taught us to be a boss. Why to earn that much what my boss decides for me, while I can be a boss and earn as much as I want. So, instead of being someone's employee you can become **self-employed.**

I know it sounds like a *one-man army*, in which you have to do everything on your own. But no, being self-employed simply means being your own boss, and that's why you're here. So, just become your own boss at the age of 18 or 19 to understand how a professional businessman thinks. Because it's not something you can read, or your teachers can teach you, it's something which will come to know only after when you decide to step in the real world or we can say in the market.

Now there might be a question arising in your mind, "*should I start my own business?*"

Well, the answer is YES as well as NO.

Now, I need you to understand why I've used both the opposite words together. It's because, you have to start your business but not really yours. Since, you are a teenager or at your early 20's and I believe you don't have that much money and manpower to start something really big and of course you don't have any business experience. But still there is something out in the market which will give you the opportunity of earning while learning. Which can be started by only the amount, you get as your pocket money and earn huge remunerations, and of course you can learn some marketing skills to become market ready within two years.

Sounds great right? But what is it? Why it's so awesome?

3. The Business

Have you ever done advertisement of something? Sure, you did. For an example, whenever you ate something delicious from somewhere, you tell your friends to go and eat from there; indirectly you are advertising their product, which is called *mouth to mouth promotion*. But, have you ever got any kind of reward from the owner for helping them in selling their product?

No, but what if you'll get paid for doing the same thing? Yeah, I know that will be great. But the question is who will pay you? And of course, how? But before anything else, let me tell you "*what it is?*"

Have you ever seen or heard about the "refer and earn apps?" Like *PayPal*, *Hike* etc. The motive of the business is basically the same as the apps. The companies want to spread their products just by doing *mouth to mouth promotion* of the products. It is usually called *Direct Selling*.
It is known as direct selling because the companies sell their products directly to the consumers. They don't give their products to the retailers, or distributors to sell them. That is also called *Network Marketing*, *Multi-Level Marketing* (MLM), *Referral Marketing* etc.

But before going any further let me tell you about the history of the business.

Let's go back in early 20th Century, Carl F. Rehnborg, while living in china, he got to know about the power of plant-based diet. In his travelling throughout China, he studied the nutritional habits of people who lived in larger cities, versus the people who lived in rural areas. He noticed an important difference in health of people between these two places.

He found the villagers are much healthier than the people lived in cities, because people who lived in cities ate more fat, sugar and salt, while on the other hand people lived in villages ate more fruits, fresh vegetables and plant products in their diet.

From the experiments and observations, Carl identified an important and unknown compound which he called *associated food factors*. He understood that people who lacked these *associated food factors* in their diets were not eating enough fruits and vegetables. Later, during political unrest in Shanghai in 1927, Carl was confined with other expatriates in camps where food was scarce. He supplemented his meager diet with crude soups he made using available grasses and plants, along with ground-up animal bones for calcium, and even rusty nails for iron.

Carl returned to the United States with an idea: What if there were supplement that could provide all the vitamins, minerals and associated food factors lacking in people's daily diets?

In 1934, he set up his own business and introduced the first multi-vitamin supplement for sale in North America. He called it Vita-6. Then in 1939 he renamed his company to *Nutrilite*

Products, Inc. After Six years, in around 1945 he used the MLM technique for the first time to boost up the sales. In which he made distributors by selling them the products and then started giving commission to the distributors for doing the same thing. Basically, he was making the consumer a new seller. So, this is how the business actually started. And now it has become one of the best sources of passive income generator and only this industry had made most of the billionaires in the world. And still it's doing the same.

But nowadays many MLM companies are out there and of course they use different plans for compensating the commissions. The most common plan that almost 90% of the companies are using is the *Binary Plan*. In this plan you will get two main business organizations in common terms we call them *legs*. So, basically you have two legs and you can add only two new distributors directly in those legs. And the distributors you add in your legs are called to be your downline. If you have more than two people to make distributors, you have to place them in your downline's leg. And for getting the commission you have to maintain the ratio of 2:1 or 1:2. This means, you must have 2 distributors in one leg and 1 in the other.

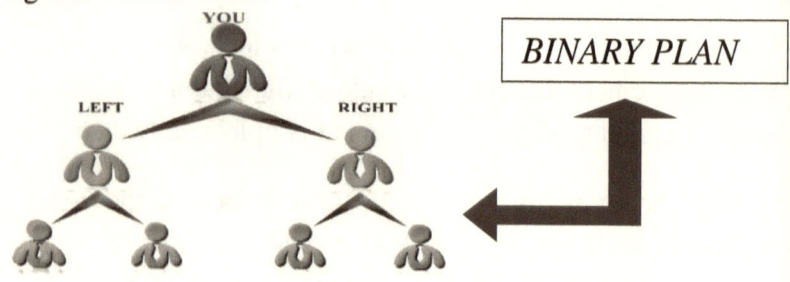

If you ask that who is going to give you the commission then the answer is; the founder of the company is going to give you the shares in the form of the commission. You might be thinking that why did I called it a business then? I know that it might sound like a job and I agree too that initially you have to work like a job but after some time you'll have a network of people working for you and then you don't need to work and that's why we call it a business; a *BUSINESS OF PEOPLE.*

4. Is it right

People often ask me the question that "Is it legal?"

Believe me it's 100% legal. Because, if this is called to be an illegal act then every shop and every selling company is illegal.

Tell me one thing, what is the process of purchasing something? First, you go to the store, ask the shopkeeper for the stuff you're looking for, you take it and in return you pay them the amount, right? And then, it's not the shopkeeper's headache what you are going to do with the product you buy, whether you eat it, sell it or just dump it in the dustbin.

Similarly, the direct selling companies are working. The only difference is they will make you use and sell their products. Like, first they'll make you buy the products and then they'll ask you to use the products as well and then they will ask you to promote or resell the products. And for that they will pay you revenue in the form of commission.

But it would be an illegal act if they will ask you to give your money for nothing and then they will ask you to do the same to others. But it's never going to happen, because the motive of the business is to spread their products massively and for that they must sell something. So, my friend Network Marketing is **NOT** illegal. And if it comes to legality then let me tell you that in countries like Europe 40-50% people are doing network marketing that means almost half a country is doing this and it doesn't make any sense that 40% people of a country are doing something illegal.

And one more thing, from now onwards *University of Delhi* has started teaching about the *Direct Selling Industry*. So, in short government of India is now started promoting Network Marketing.

5. Why to do

If entrepreneurship is the only option, then I can create my own *YouTube* channel or Website or even I can build and develop my own apps. Even these are the sources of passive income too, then why should I do network marketing?

Let me tell you, that I also live in 21st century and I know what websites and YouTube channels are and I'm not even saying that you are wrong or something. But there are some extra benefits (except the passive income) of doing network marketing instead of these.

First of all, unlike web designing and app development it doesn't require any education. That means the people who are not educated enough can do it too because you don't need any degree to use a product. So, you can consider it as a benefit too and unlike jobs there's no age limit you can do it any time, but I'll suggest you start it at the age of 18 or 19. And of course, you need investment for creating an app; like if you want to develop an app you need to know coding or if you are thinking to hire a developer then my friend no one is going to do it for free. Beside that Network Marketing teach you ethics, I'm repeating again that Network Marketing or MLM teach you ethics, they will inject discipline in your habits. It will provide you a virtual successful environment because it works on the theory of "*FAKE IT TILL YOU MAKE IT*". And unlike any other businesses this is the only one which gives importance to the training. In other businesses you'll never get any help or support from anyone but here you can ask for help anytime from your up-lines/seniors. And the best part is that they will never suggest you anything wrong because if your business ruins then theirs will also be in trouble. So, you can trust them blindly.

Another point is that every industry has to go through four different phases; Negative Phase, Positive Phase, Growth Phase and Competition Phase. Let me give you an example, do you know when the banks were introduced in India for the first time, people thought that they are fraud because basically bank says deposit your money here and we will give you interest on that. So, people thought that they were trying to fool them and if they gave them the money, they will run away with that. So that was the negative phase of the bank industry but slowly and gradually banks came into the positive phase and from positive phase they entered in the growth phase in no time and I don't think that I have to tell you about the competition phase because there are many banks offering different plans competing for proving themselves the best. Like banks Network Marketing industry is also in its Negative Phase in India because Indians are still running behind the government jobs. It will be best to join a Network Marketing company in its Negative Phase because whenever it enters in its positive phase your growth will be guaranteed and this industry had made many billionaires even being in the Negative Phase, so just think what will happen if it enters in its positive phase.

There's good news for you, according to **FICCI** (*Federation of Indian Chambers of Commerce and Industry*) the Direct Selling or Network Marketing industry is going to reach the worth of ₹**64,500 Billion Crores** by 2025 in India. It already has the market size of over 180 billion USD.

> What is the future of direct sale in India?
>
> **Direct** selling, one of the oldest and traditional forms of selling, is likely to reach Rs. 64,500 crore billion in **India** by 2025, a FICCI-KPMG report said on Tuesday. **Direct** selling has already emerged as a successful industry in over 100 countries, with a market size of USD 180 billion.

It is said that Network Marketing is the business of 21st century but in India there are only 0.7% people who are doing Network Marketing this time and majority of them are successful. Think of the time when the number increases, what will be your growth then.

There are many other benefits of doing Network Marketing like it will help you in developing your Personality, Communication Skills, Management skills, Leadership skills, convincing skills, influencing skills etc. And I think these are the enough reasons for investing your time in Network Marketing. Because people pay in institutes for developing these skills and here these things are considered as extra benefits.

After all you will become financially free and independent in just three years because you would have made a successful network that means you can take your retirement at the age of 25 and your only work will be, to conduct seminars or training sessions because you have initially invested your precious time here in this industry. Successful people often says that "*No one do Network Marketing by their choice, people do it by chance*" but trust me my friend once you enter in this field with a focused mindset you'll never regret.

6. Conclusion

People often say if you really want to enjoy your life it's better to work hard at your early 20's. But we take this statement in a different way we think that working hard at this stage means studying hard but no my friend it means you must do something smart and if you ask me then I'm going to suggest you to do network marketing. People often ask me, *if it is so good then why everyone is not doing this*? Then the answer is people are crazy and lazy as well. Everyone is not doing this because people are afraid of doing difficult things, they want comfort and they don't want to leave their comfort zone. Everybody wants to be treated like a celebrity, but they don't want to work hard like they worked in their starting days, why? The reason is very simple; they don't want to leave their comfort zone. You have to understand that today's comfort will destroy all your dreams. So just get up and start working for your dreams.

There are many Network Marketing companies out there, but the main problem is to choose the best out of them. So, there are some points you have to keep in mind while choosing the right company like,

1. What are the products? Products should be something worthy and salable, like if they ask you to sell movie tickets then leave that company and also tell them about the *Book my show* app.

2. What is the mindset of people of the company? Do they only talk about money or profit? If it is so, then definitely you will not going to learn anything.

3. Did they really give importance to the training? One of the most important points you must observe that how do they work? How many times they organize a training session? The training sessions must be organized at least once or twice in a month.

At the end all I want to say that working harder and smarter at the right age is far better than the jobs after studying because it is not going to give you the boon of early retirement. Why I'm asking to retire soon? Because early retirement with a source of passive income makes you do whatever you want to do. In simple words you can fully enjoy your life and you can spend as much time as you want with your family and friends. So, it's your life and of course it's totally your decision, just take it wisely because your one decision will change your and your entire family's current status. And if you want to ask someone about the industry then please ask someone who at least did Network Marketing **HONESTLY**.

www.ingramcontent.com/pod-product-compliance
Lightning Source LLC
Chambersburg PA
CBHW030032250526
45464CB00025B/1368